that's my boy

Jose Luis Cortes

that's my boy

English version by
John Medcalf

Collins

Collins Liturgical Publications
187 Piccadilly, London W1V 9DA

Collins Liturgical Australia
55 Clarence St, Sydney 2000 PO Box 3023 Sydney 2001

ISBN 0 00 599796 8

Originally published in Spanish by Promocion Popular Cristiana, Madrid
© PPC, 1979 © Jose Luis Cortes
First published in English 1984
© 1984 English translation William Collins Sons & Co Ltd.

English graphics by Wagner Design Unit
Made and printed in Glasgow by William Collins Sons & Co Ltd

BUT ARE YOU REALLY SURE YOU WANT US TO TELL YOU ABOUT JC?
YOU MAY BE A BIT SHOCKED
HE WASN'T AS GOOD-LOOKING AS HIS PHOTOS
IN FACT HE WAS A BIT ON THE SHORT SIDE
AND HE SPOKE WITH A SLIGHT LISP
BUT HE WAS AN INCREDIBLY NICE PERSON.....

SMALL WONDER HIS DAD
WAS ALWAYS SAYING —

that's my boy

The entire existence
of a Christian
could be said
to consist of
a return to simplicity

(IGNACIO SILONE: "The Adventure of a Poor
    Christian")

WELL IT ALL BEGAN WHEN HE WAS STILL LITTLE MORE THAN A LAD......

family photos

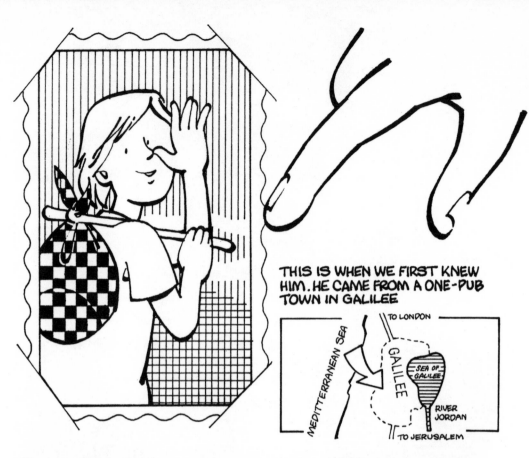

THIS IS WHEN WE FIRST KNEW HIM. HE CAME FROM A ONE-PUB TOWN IN GALILEE

HE AND HIS FATHER RAN A BUILDERS YARD. THERE ARE NO PHOTOS OF HIS FATHER BECAUSE HE DIED WHEN JC WAS STILL YOUNG, BEFORE PHOTOS WERE INVENTED.

WHAT WE DO HAVE IS THIS DRAWING WHICH JC HIMSELF DID WHILE STILL AT NURSERY SCHOOL. HE CALLED IT "MY FAMILY" BUT WHO CAN TELL WHICH IS HIS FATHER?

WHAT A WOMAN! SHE USED TO ORGANISE CHRISTMAS PARTIES FOR THE HANDICAPPED, COACH-TRIPS FOR THE OLD AGE PENSIONERS, AND IN HER SPARE TIME SHE WROTE SONGS - THE BEST KNOWN IS THAT PROTEST SONG ABOUT THE HAVES AND HAVE-NOTS WHICH BEGINS —

THOSE PEOPLE WHO WERE NOT CONTENT TO STAGGER
THROUGH LIFE FROM ONE RUM AND COKE TO THE
NEXT ASKED HIM :

WELL JOHNNY, WHAT MUST WE DO ?

JB answered:

THE TIME HAS COME TO STOP
BEING PHONEY AND TO ASK
OURSELVES WHERE WE'RE
GOING........

THOSE WHO AGREE WITH ME JUMP IN THE WATER!

THIS PHOTO IS A BIT HAZY, BECAUSE THE SUN DID SOMETHING SPECIAL WHEN JC PLUNGED INTO THE WATER.
IT WAS AS IF GOD HIMSELF HAD FLOODED THE WHOLE JORDAN RIVER WITH LIGHT......NOT LIKE THE OLD TESTAMENT (THUNDER AND LIGHTNING, ETC.) BUT SOFTLY, GENTLY.....LIKE A DOVE....

Then JC went away.

JB's Message

Enough! I've kept quiet long enough and now I'm going to shout the truth up and down this valley for everyone to hear.

I'm fed up with politicians, priests and multinationals!

Stop leading us down fifth-rate by-ways not even marked on a good map!

Only a 10-lane highway is good enough for God — straight as a die, straight to the point, no wasting of time, no deceiving the people.

I want to be free in a free world, for God's sake!

Politicians!

Most of you are gangsters, money-grabbing and corrupt. The ordinary people despise your double-dealing and the poison in your viper tongues when you mount your election campaigns and make your empty promises.

You have degraded the noble art of government and turned the God-created science of politics into a trough of swill fit only for pigs.

Where are the high principles of a Thomas More?

Where is the single-minded, simple-minded honesty of a Gandhi?

Where is truth? Where is justice?

Where is compassion for the poor?

Priests! Prelates! Preachers of eternal truth!

The people turn to you for spiritual strength and consolation in a filthy world made filthier by opportunistic politicians.

And what do they find?

Weak straws blowing around in the wind! God help us if a gale comes along!

Luxurious living and private medical insurances... in a world where 2 out of 3 go to bed hungry and die before 45!

Where's your **faith?**

Have you made a **career** out of the most sublime of vocations on this earth?

I tell you solemnly, put all the crap of your lives on a bonfire, and burn it – now!

Stockbrokers, bankers, house-owners without a mortgage round your neck – get rid of your excess!

Share what you have with the poor!

Your riches are like the blocks of concrete used to sink the victims the mafia throws into the ocean: they'll be the death of you!

Armed Forces, Police, Prison Officers and all uniformed guardians of the peace – yours is a dangerous vocation; dangerous to others and dangerous to yourselves!

Resist the temptation to take pleasure in violence; a sadist is always a depraved and deprived creature, deserving of pity.

Don't abuse your uniforms and your weapons; be in the front line of the genuine peace marches, marching **with** the people, not against them.

Don't trade in your consciences for a quiet life and fat pensions!

(And blessed is little Costa Rica, that doesn't have an Army)

Stop being phoney!

Stop deceiving yourselves!

Ask yourselves where you're going!

It is the height of idiocy to keep repeating "I'm a son of Abraham", "I'm more Catholic than the Pope", "I'm a socialist for ever".

No, no, no!!! If God wanted to he could make the streets of Soho holier than a Trappist monastery, he could turn pimps into Bishops, he could... but that's not the point! **You** must change! He **loves** you!

He **wants** you to change!

Stop staring at the patches in my trousers – the way I dress is a protest against the sinful waste of a world divided into ever fewer 'haves' and ever more 'have-nots' (JB was the first ecologist and spoke even better than Petra Kelly)

I want to be free in a free world, for God's sake!

I'll eat what I can and when I can get it.

Too many of you make a god of your belly, enslaving yourselves instead of living free of worry. (How many centuries must we wait until Frank does his streaking act through the streets of Assisi?)

Look into the water — Look, I tell you!

You're going to see a really big fish swim up here very soon!

Any fool can stand on the bank of life and watch the water pass by!

Get in the water... get wet!

Move up-stream...

Even dead dogs can swim **with** the stream...

Go against the current... that's what life is all about!

Be different!

Be free!

Be you!

Sgd   John Baptist

it takes all sorts...

LIFE IN A SMALL TOWN DOESN'T MAKE FRONT-PAGE NEWS:

VIOLET PARKER STAYED UNMARRIED ALL HER LIFE TO LOOK AFTER HER INVALID MOTHER

ANITA AND JOY HAD AN ALCOHOLIC FATHER

OLD MR JONES WAS ALWAYS WILLING TO TALK ABOUT HIS DAYS AS A SOLDIER IN THE TRENCHES, AND HIS DEAD COMPANIONS...

.....OH, WHAT A LOVELY WAR.....

VINCENT BROWN, THE VILLAGE IDIOT, WHO WAS ALSO CROSS-EYED :

2 OR 3 TARTS WHO KEPT A PLACE ON THE OUTSKIRTS OF TOWN

DAN, WHO SOLD PERFUMES AND AFTER SHAVE.......

HAPPINESS ISN'T HAVING MORE AND MORE BUTTONS TO PRESS

GOD'S IDEAL HOME IS NOT NECCESSARILY THE ONE IN THE GLOSSY MAGAZINES.

Because JC didn't have an account with the Chase Nazareth Bank, Dan ("Lily Marlene After-shave") called him a dreamer, and because he laughed in the synagogue Rabbi Lefebrini said the Bishop wouldn't confirm him, and when he yawned at the political meetings the Trots called him a "reactionary".

BUT JC USED TO TELL HIS MOTHER—"THATS NOT WHAT IT'S ALL ABOUT, MUM!"

AND MARY GOODE, THE PRIDE AND JOY OF NAZARETH, USED TO AGREE : "NO, THAT'S NOT REAL LIFE AT ALL!"

A FAREWELL LETTER

Dear Mum,

When you wake up I'll already have gone. I hate goodbyes, and you've suffered enough because of me.

It's night-time now while I'm writing, and the cat is looking at me as if to say "Can't anyone get a bit of honest sleep in this house any more?"

I want to explain why I'm leaving you and why I'm not going to carry on making door-frames and straightening out chairs for the rest of my life.

For 30 years now I've been watching the people of our town and I've tried to understand what makes them tick, what makes them get up every morning, and what they dream of at night.

Dan in the perfume-shop, and half the town's population with him, just dream of getting rich and seem to think that the more things they have in life the more fulfilled they'll be. The Mayor and his bunch are in love with power, and just want to order around more and more people. The Rabbi and his fan-club have called a halt in their lives to any effort to grow and develop, and they pretend this is the Will of God.

As a result of all this, most days in Nazareth are too grey, and the loneliness too great, to be borne by normal people. There is not enough joy in life, there is too much petty bitterness.

Sometimes, Mother, when the postman brought letters from faraway relations and the people rushed up to him with HOPE written big all over their faces, hoping for good news from anyone anywhere, I wanted to shout aloud to them all -

THE GOOD NEWS IS ALREADY HERE!

THE KINGDOM OF GOD IS WITHIN YOU!

THE BEST LETTERS ARE INSIDE YOU!

WHY DO YOU SAY YOU ARE LAME WHEN

GOD HAS GIVEN YOU LEGS OF GAZELLES?

I feel caught up by the fulness of life, Mother. I feel
a fire inside me, burning me up to tell people simple and
beautiful news that the newspapers never publish. And I'd
like to burn the world with this fire, so that in every
tiny corner there is life, yes - life in abundance.
I know I'm just a carpenter, without any Higher Education, and
that I'm only just old enough to open my mouth in public. But
I don't want to wait any longer, to be "more mature", or take my
Degree in Theology.....and this afternoon I heard that they've
taken JB prisoner, the JB who used to baptise in the River
Jordan, you remember?

Now that JB has gone, who is left to fan the small flame of
hope still in the hearts of the poor? Who will dare to shout
the truth in a world full of lies and propaganda? Who will
tell those people who are simple-hearted and long-suffering
that they have a right to live because they've been loved
since the beginning of the universe?

There is too much unhappiness, Mother, for me to be content
making rocking-chairs for a few customers. Too many people
are blind, handicapped, poor - for them this world is a
blasphemy against God's love. Nobody can believe in God
in a world where people die and are unhappy... at least
without being on the side of those who give up their lives
so that this won't continue, so that the world becomes what
God wanted it to become.

To be honest, I don't know very clearly what I'm going to do.
I know where I'll begin... but I don't know where it will
all end. I'm going to begin in Capernaum, on the lakeside,
where there are more people than in Nazareth.

It's getting light now. I'll write to you. I'll come and
see you from time to time. The neighbours, the cat, the
stars and God Himself will keep you company in that great
brotherhood and sisterhood of Nature that we human beings
are incapable of fully discovering.

And when we've succeeded in forming a small group of people
to live and love as we're supposed to live and love, then
you can come and join us, blessed among all the women of
Israel, full of grace, full of flowers and music, all of
which you gave to me.

X

Your Jesus

AND SO IT WAS THAT IN NAZARETH (JUST LIKE ANYWHERE ELSE IN THE WORLD) THERE WERE PEOPLE WITH A WEAKNESS FOR MONEY, POWER, RELIGION, ETC. BUT WHAT ABOUT THE REST, THOSE LEFT OVER? JC MADE FRIENDS WITH THESE 'LEFT-OVERS!' (AFTER ALL, HE AND HIS FAMILY BELONGED TO THE LEFT-OVERS, THE REMNANT, OF ISRAEL).

the gang

Capernaum, on the shore of the Lake of Galilee, was a more important place than Nazareth, with a more sophisticated atmosphere.

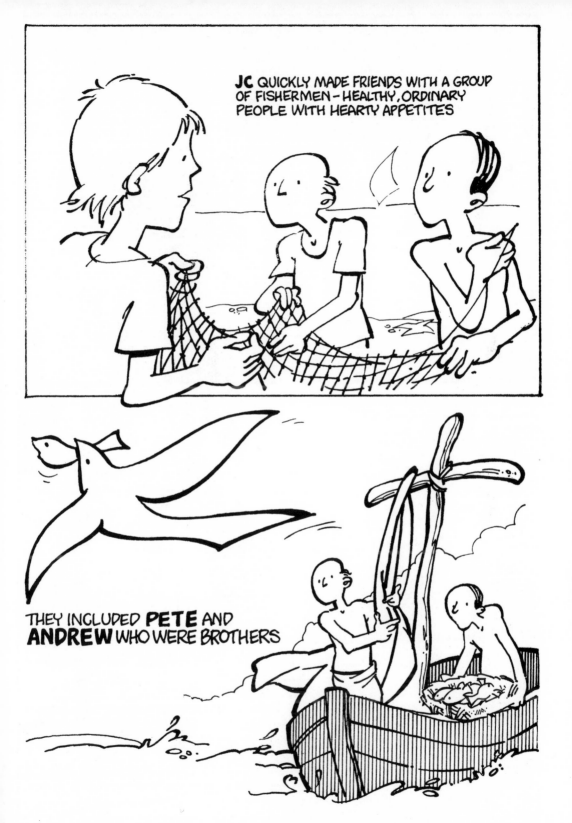

Jim and John Thunderson, also brothers, were always putting up
anti-government posters in the night time........

AFTER A FEW WEEKS WE WERE ALREADY A KIND OF GANG, AND WE HAD A FEELING THAT THINGS WERE GOING TO GET A LOT BETTER

NATURALLY WE DIDN'T ALL AGREE ON HOW THINGS WOULD GET BETTER —

LET'S START BY EACH KILLING A ROMAN....

YOU WATCH TOO MUCH TV, KID

WE'VE GOT TO ENJOY LIFE AS WELL. WE COULD FORM A POP GROUP AND GO ROUND SINGING GOSPEL SONGS LIKE CLIFF RICHARD!

At nighttime, after work, they all went to Pete and Deirdre's house, and talked and discussed things until well after midnight.

WHO SAYS THERE AREN'T ENOUGH OF US TO CHANGE THIS TOWN AND THIS COUNTRY? YOU COULD SAY THE SAME ABOUT A WOMAN WHEN SHE PUTS YEAST INTO THE DOUGH...

Just this pathetic little bit to make all that flour rise?

But then.....

FLOUR

THE COMING OF GOD'S KINGDOM MEANS THAT HUMAN BEINGS WON'T BE ASHAMED TO LIVE!

MORE AND MORE PEOPLE FROM CAPERNAUM BEGAN TO COME ALONG TO THESE INFORMAL DISCUSSIONS, AND GRADUALLY A NEW SPIRIT COULD BE NOTICED IN THE TOWN : ONE BOAT-CREW HELPING ANOTHER FOR EXAMPLE, AND EVERYONE TAKING THE TRADE-UNION MORE SERIOUSLY ; PETE ALLOWED HIS 2 CHILDREN TO GO TO SCHOOL, INSTEAD OF SAYING THAT EDUCATION WAS ONLY FOR THE RICH, AS HE USED TO . . . . .

THE FACT IS
THAT WHEN PEOPLE GET TOGETHER AND DISCUSS THINGS SERIOUSLY, MIRACLES CAN HAPPEN, WELL ALMOST MIRACLES— AT LEAST THE BEGINNINGS OF HOPE.

The Speed of the convoy is the speed of the slowest ship...

The undersigned members of JC's Christian Commune want to make it absolutely clear that many of the later descriptions of what we were like are a pain in the neck.

It has been said, for instance, that to belong to our community it was necessary to flee from the world or make perpetual vows, that we had to undergo certain initiation rites (taking cold showers, eating raw meat and other horrible things). It has even been suggested that we met together to discuss how many natures there were in Christ. Any normal person will know that this is all ridiculous for people working an 8-hour day.

For this reason we think it a good idea at this point to describe some of our members (apart from the better-known ones like Pete and John, etc), so that you can see what sort of people belonged to this "Community of the Kingdom" as we called ourselves.

For example:

LEN was a priest who had his failings, but he had one big quality: he gave all his energy to the defence and protection of the poor. When he got married some of the parish gossips said "Yes, we could see it coming!" but there was no lack of wine at his wedding-reception, because JC himself was there.

MARILYN lost her first husband in a traffic accident and got married again because her 4 children needed a father. This second husband turned out to be a drunkard and made her suffer a lot. But her children turned out well.

EUGENE was only 15 when his father abandoned the family, and Eugene had to leave school and go to work in a cement factory so as to keep the family afloat. He'll never abandon his family and is determined his own children will go to University if they wish to.

B. CLARKE used to sleep with a prostitute now and again (always the same one, but she was certainly a prostitute). He did it through necessity, because his wife was dying of cancer and he nursed her right up to the end, trusting that God will keep her alive for him on the other side.

LARRY was a homosexual who killed himself eventually by an overdose of something. He now rests — at last — in peace. He preferred the judgement of God to the judgement — morning, afternoon, and night — of his neighbours.

KATE worked like a dozen men, and still had time to attend her Street Residents' Committee until all hours of the night. She was an atheist, but God knew her well.

EILEEN who was blind

MIKE who used to sing sad sentimental ballads about orphans and widows and wars. One day he died, without ever having changed his tune. He'll be in good hands now.

LUKE, LEWIS, MARTIN, NANCY and others who were CND supporters.

RUDY was a priest, like Len, and — like Len — had his problems. When he was 45 he had the courage to re-examine his personal faith from top to bottom during a week's retreat. He finished absolutely shattered and practically without any faith at all. But when he came back, the community gave him a big embrace and wished him "shalom".

PAUL I remember, talking of Rudy, was a priest who got to 81 and died in his cassock. Some of his ideas where prehistoric, but he always had a great sense of humour, which probably saved him. Talking of 80-year olds, there was old **LIZ** full of wrinkles and with snow-white hair. She smoked and drank up till the end. She always called us "dear children", perhaps because her own children — a son and a daughter — were ashamed of her and never visited her. She always felt at home with us.

VALERIE young, good-looking and very nervous. She got worked up over nothing at all. Religion only ever gave her scruples and worries but she carried on her search for peace. She worked in a flower-shop, and one Christmas she brought in a pink hyacinth, put it on the altar and started to cry. She was a case!

JACKY had the mind of a child, although he was an adult. He went round in a wheelchair and was in a pitiful state. It was he who 'converted' Julia, the village gossip, that day when she went up to him and wiped his nose clean. It may seem unimportant, but it wasn't so for us...

IN ADDITION there were lots of children, a youth group, as well as a group of teenagers like Eugene who met to discuss whether masturbation was a sin or not, and whether dating girls was the only important thing in life... and so many others as well, because the above-mentioned are only an example.

90% would probably have left the group if we'd made Sunday church-going an obligation. 80% couldn't have said whether they had "faith" or not, and even less could they say whether they believed each and every one of the teachings of the Church.

But for everybody, meeting up with JC was a discovery — even for poor Larry. We came to understand that to be human was the best way to begin to become gods. We also discovered that somebody always loves us, even though we begin to go downhill once we're 30. We learned that when you walk you sometimes trip, but that walking is the surest way of getting anywhere.

They were marvellous people, with lots of heart and humanity. I still remember one of the manifestos of the commune which we formed; it finished with the words —

People of courage throughout the world unite!

AND SO EVERYTHING WAS GOING ALONG VERY WELL IN OUR COMMUNITY UNTIL (O WICKED WORLD!) THE PHARISEES DECIDED TO POKE THEIR NOSES INTO OUR AFFAIRS . . . . .

What really put his back up
was to see how they'd turned
religion into something official

and that some people
pretended to have God in their pockets

and others said that the Church was one thing
and real life was another

AT THE BEGINNING, THE PHARISEES WERE
CONTENT TO WAG THEIR POISONOUS TONGUES

HOW CAN HE BE A 'SAINT' IF HE PLAYS CENTRE-FORWARD FOR CAPERNAUM ROVERS?

HAVEN'T YOU SEEN HOW HE CAN'T RESIST FISH-AND-CHIPS WITH PICKLED ONIONS?

....THEY BEGAN TO FRIGHTEN THE SIMPLE PEOPLE
WITH STORIES OF HELL-FIRE AND DAMNATION
IF THEY DIDN'T FOLLOW THEIR OLD-FASHIONED VIEWS ON RELIGION....

THEIR KIND OF RELIGION HAS PRODUCED:

Huge cathedrals that look like palaces for the rich

Neurotic visionaries in need of a psychiatrist

frightened young people who see atheism as freedom from fear

a society that associates religion with the most reactionary political parties

etc...

as a personal exercise -
write down some of the hang-ups that a "religious upbringing" has given you

....
....
....

WELL, I'M TELLING YOU*: YOUR GAME IS UP!

it will be taken away from you and given to those who will produce better results

LIT.'VERILY, VERILY I SAY UNTO YOU....

YOU AND YOUR LAWS AND RULES! YOU PROTEST IN A RESTAURANT ABOUT A GREASE-SPOT, AND THEN YOU GULP DOWN YOUR FIZZY DRINK OR YOUR INSTANT COFFEE WITHOUT THINKING HOW THESE MULTINATIONAL COMPANIES ARE STRANGLING THE ECONOMIES OF THE 3rd WORLD

YOU CALL DIVINE LAW WHAT IS NOTHING MORE THAN A LOT OF HUMAN CUSTOMS AND TRADITIONS PILED UP OVER THE CENTURIES.

NO, MY FRIENDS. THAT'S NOT WHAT IT'S ALL ABOUT. GO AND MEDITATE ABOUT WHAT GOD REALLY SAID:

I don't want laws;
I want love

He's a God not
of the dead
but of the <u>living</u>

In the end JC just let them go.

Later on in the pub when we were just ourselves, he'd tell us.....

BEWARE OF RELIGIOUS PROFESSIONALISM:

DON'T BE A DO-GOODER JUST TO FEEL GOOD AFTERWARDS

IF YOU GET BAGS UNDER THE EYES THROUGH WORKING FOR OTHERS, DISGUISE THEM WITH EYE-SHADOW

BE SIMPLE AND SINCERE WHEN YOU PRAY: JUST AS IF YOU WERE SPEAKING WITH CHILDREN

BY THE WAY, I REMEMBER A STORY HE TOLD US ONE DAY:

"2 men go to a church to pray.
The first is a stockbroker, and his
prayer runs more or less like this:

Thanks, Lord, for making me a success-story.
I've donated $2,000 to the Cathedral
Restoration Fund. I have an ideal Christian
family, and I never gamble or smoke.

WELL THE STOCKBROKER WENT BANKRUPT AND THE DROPOUT WON TOP PRIZE IN THE POOLS
I REMEMBER A DIFFERENT ENDING
WELL, YOU KNOW WHAT I MEAN........
IN OTHER WORDS, IT WAS'NT SO MUCH THAT JC WAS ANTI-CHURCH, BUT RATHER THE CHURCH AT THE TIME WASN'T BIG ENOUGH TO CONTAIN PEOPLE LIKE JC.

"I Dream of a Church"

LYRIC
by Simon P. Johnson

(No rights reserved - just give a coin to the Fishermen's Benevolent Society or the Royal Lifeboat Society)

I dream of a Church
where love and people
are more important
than stone and steeple

I dream of a Church
with an open door
where no one is privileged
except the poor

I dream of a Church
where milk and honey
will flow more freely
than power and money

I dream of a Church
where young and old
will be inspired
to change their world

I dream of a Church
that will make my dreams come true

love is a many-splendored thing

He'd grown up in a small town, he'd lived for 30 years like any other working person and he felt at home with ordinary people

THE PEOPLE LIKED HIM IN A SPECIAL WAY THAT'S HARD TO DESCRIBE—

well the boy took a turn for the better and was soon running around

And it was almost the same story with Pete Stone's mother-in-law.

JUST THEN THE CHILD THREW A FIT, AND FROZE STIFF.
PEOPLE SAID HE WAS DEAD, BUT **JC** SLAPPED HIS FACE AND
SAID:

No wonder JC was getting a reputation as a wonder-worker.........

WHAT REALLY SADDENS ME IS SEEING SO MUCH SUFFERING. I DO WHAT I CAN TO HELP, AND IF THEY GET BETTER THEN THANK GOD FOR THAT.

BUT JC REALLY HIT THE JACKPOT AT A PLACE CALLED NAIM.

Naim is a small village not far from Nazareth, and we were passing through on our way back from a weekend in the country.....when suddenly we met up with a funeral procession.....

It was a terrible sight to see that funeral procession.
Katie was crying and sobbing like an Irish Sunday,
her eyes all red so that she could hardly see
anything.

We all kept on the other side of the road;
after all, it wasn't any of our business.....

BUT JC WENT UP TO THE MOTHER, AND JUST SAID TO HER:

DON'T CRY, KATIE ....

IN FACT WE WERE ALL CRYING; EVEN JC HAD TEARS, RUNNING DOWN HIS CHEEKS!

SOME CALLED IT A MIRACLE. OTHERS SAID IT WAS TELEPATHY OR WITCHCRAFT OR SOMETHING LIKE THAT....WHATEVER IT WAS, EVERYONE STOPPED CRYING AND SEAN WENT UP TO KATIE AND SAID SIMPLY—

mum, i'm thirsty.

NAIM IS A ONE-HORSE PLACE NEAR NAZARETH, BUT I THINK WE MENTIONED THAT BEFORE.

112

BUT EVERY MORNING HE WOULD READ THE COURT CASES IN THE DAILY PAPER, AFRAID THAT ONE DAY HIS SON WOULD TURN UP ON PAGE 5 OR 6

MEANWHILE THE YOUNG SON WAS LIVING IT UP IN THE BIG CITY. FIRST HE SPENT ALL HIS GIRL-FRIEND'S MONEY, THEN HE LEFT HER HANGING DRY. NEXT, HE WROTE TO HIS FATHER ASKING FOR MONEY, AND SEVERAL TIMES HIS FATHER ANSWERED, SENDING A LETTER WITH THE CHEQUE. THE SON WOULD THROW AWAY THE LETTER UNREAD AND CASH THE CHEQUE. HIS FATHER LATER DECIDED NOT TO SEND ANY MORE MONEY.

MUCH LATER ON, THE SON GOT A PART-TIME JOB IN A LAUNDERETTE.

BUT HIS FATHER SAW HIM FROM THE OTHER SIDE OF THE HIGH ST AND RUSHED OVER WITHOUT CARING ABOUT THE TRAFFIC.......

HE GAVE HIS SON A BIG HUG —

You've lost weight, my boy. Do you know, your dog has slept on your bed every night, waiting for you to come home?

THE SON STARTED TO SPEAK

DAD, I'M SOR......

BUT HIS FATHER WOULD'NT ALLOW HIM TO GO ON

WHY DON'T WE GO DOWN TO THE LOCAL TONIGHT FOR A GAME OF DARTS AND A FEW BEERS!

BUT THEN THE OLDER SON TURNED UP—THE ONE WHO WAS STUDYING LAW

WASN'T HE A VET?

Dad, you're spoiling that boy. You're just not behaving in a responsible manner.

Somebody else can punish him—I'm his father

AND THAT EVENING THE 2 OF THEM WENT TO THE GEORGE AND DRAGON ON THEIR OWN (THE ELDER BROTHER SAID HE HAD SOME CHEMISTRY TO DO)

—WASN'T IT LAW HE WAS STUDYING?

—WHAT DOES IT MATTER? DON'T BE SO PERNICKETY.

THE GOOD

Here you see our honest Fred
Who's not ashamed to earn his bread.

And these are skinheads looking for a fight....
They see Fred Rock-a-Billy coming into sight.

So they slash him with a bike-chain
and leave him half-dead

Along comes a vicar
and pokes out his head.....

pops it back in again
when he sees poor Fred

Albert and Joan are driving back home
One look at Fred and it's full-speed ahead!

RASTAFARIAN

Rasta Ralph from Railton Road
(unemployed, no fixed abode)

arrives to see the skinheads' crime
and saves poor Fred in the nick of time.

He gently takes Fred on his back
and then they're off to see the quack

The quack demands to see Ralph's money
(No NHS in those days, sonny)

So Rasta Ralph is stony broke
but deep down he's a happy bloke

The moral is: a friend in need
is ten times better than a creed

JC was like his Mother in this respect - he was convinced that the best specimens of the human race were the ordinary, simple people who weren't worried about keeping up with the Joneses, but only with keeping up their peckers when faced with problems.

THE PHILOSOPHERS AND POLITICIANS HAVE GIVEN US IDEAS AND THEORIES ABOUT THE WORLD, BUT FROM NOW ON PEOPLE OF GOODWILL MUST <u>CHANGE</u> THE WORLD.

DIAMONDS GIVE BIRTH TO NOTHING, WHEREAS MANURE PRODUCES LILIES.

So it's not surprising that **JC** was always in "bad" company - alcoholics, drug-addicts, gays, whores, epileptics, etc.

He understood unmarried mothers, sympathised with problem drinkers. He was overcome by clear, honest eyes, and when he saw eyes clouded with envy and hatred, he would ask "Why?"

He was always forgiving people. He said that if you love a lot you deserve to have a lot of things forgiven.

Old Emily couldn't stop herself
shouting out one day —

127

More of the same:

A Story Many of the people used to criticise JC for knowing all the pubs and prostitutes by their names. But he used to say: "I know it's not the ideal, but then it's not the Olympic athletes who need to see a doctor, but those who can't live without their vallium or their sleeping-pills. In any case, it breaks my heart just to see them so helpless...

'Suppose you had ten children (**real** children) and one night was after midnight and one of them hadn't come home. It gets to 2am, 3am, – wouldn't you leave the other 9 kids safely in bed and go out looking for the tenth? I don't believe any real parent would say to himself "Oh well, I've got nine safe and sound; I'll forget the tenth". Of course they wouldn't.

'In other words, I'm obviously not saying it's **wrong** to be a good person. I'm just worried that nobody wants to look after the others'.

A Miracle Jericho was in a green, fertile valley; it was fabulously beautiful. Sometimes we used to go there, because it wasn't too far from Jerusalem.
One day, just outside the town, there was a blind man sitting at the roadside –

– What's all the noise and fuss about, he asked, when we were walking past.

– We're from Nazareth, and we like to visit Jericho sometimes, because it's so beautiful and green.

– It's alright for you. I'm blind; I don't know what green is, or red, or blue.

– Green is like the soft rain in April, red is like a kiss on the lips, blue is like a symphony by Beethoven.

– Don't rub it in, then.

— Wouldn't you like to see all these lovely colours?

— You bet I would. I'm sick & tired of the black midnight that goes on for ever and ever and... (All of a sudden he started crying.) (There's bound to be some expert exegete who'll say it was the crying that made him see again — what does it matter?)

And just as we were going he gave a great yell —

— Your shirt is as white as the light of God! (when you've **always** been able to see, you don't say things like that, and you're always finding fault with things — you see the grease-spots on your friend's coat, or you can see smuts on people's faces... and so on)

Another story: One day we were talking about the Cup Final, when there was a fearful din and racket. A crowd of men were dragging along a women who was crying and shouting to be freed. Her hair was all dishevelled and her clothes had been torn.

They all stopped in front of us. A school-teacher stepped out in front and said to JC:

— Alright then, Mr Heartstrings. What do you say to this! This women teaches in a Christian School, and she has seduced one of the pupils. The poor boy is only 15, and she's obviously the one to blame; she's old enough to be his mother. We're taking her along to a School Governors' Board, where she'll be sacked on the spot. Then we are going to report her to the police and finally to the newspaper reporters. Her name will be mud in this town...

JC was silent. He always hated seeing women ill-treated by men, and he seemed to be nervously drawing graffiti in the dust with a stick. Then —

— Stop playing around with that stick and give us a straight answer. Are we right or wrong?

So then JC looked up and spoke.

— There's another way of looking at the problem, gentlemen. Let the person who believes he has a clean conscience be the first to call in the gutter press.

(Boy, you should have seen that crowd of chauvinistic pigs when JC said that! They didn't know where to look. One by one they crept off, until only the woman teacher remained.)

JC stopped his doodling in the dust and looked up at her,

— What's up, my dear? Did they change their minds?

— Yes, it seems so, Mr Heartstrings (she thought that was really his name!)

—Alright then, I can't condemn you either.
But think very carefully before you do such a thing again, won't you? God bless you.

JC had behaved like a real gentleman, don't you think? All the same, the woman later had to leave the town, because they made life impossible for her.

Another story They once sent 3 police-constables to arrest him, at the time things were beginning to get serious. The coppers stood listening to him for a good while, then they went back to the Police-Station empty-handed. When the Sergeant asked why they hadn't arrested JC, one of them said:

Go and listen to him speaking!
If **he** deserves to be arrested, then **we** deserve to be shot.
Needless to say they were all punished and lost their jobs.
But they didn't lose their souls.

I hope it's all come over clearly how JC stressed the importance of having a good heart, putting your heart in the right place as we say.

I hope also you've understood that the people who most mattered for him were the children, the sick, the poor, the defenceless. These are the ones, he used to say, who'll live one day in mansions.

This last bit is so important that it deserves a special chapter...

poor power rules

OK

NOWADAYS YOU CAN SEE **JC**'S NAME WRITTEN UP OVER SUMPTUOUS CHURCHES, OR CRUCIFIXES MADE OF THE MOST EXPENSIVE MATERIALS, RICH PEOPLE CALLING THEIR OWN PROJECTS THE "WORK OF GOD", etc

...BUT **JC** WASN'T LIKE THAT AT ALL. HE WOULD NEVER HAVE ENTERED A CHURCH WHERE YOU NEEDED A SUIT AND TIE TO WORSHIP GOD.

HE WOULD HAVE DESPISED A BISHOP WHO ATE BETTER THAN THE POOREST OF HIS FLOCK...

NOWADAYS PEOPLE DRESS UP JC IN GOLDEN ROBES AND PUT JEWELLED CROWNS ON MARY'S HEAD (AS IF SHE WERE A CARNIVAL QUEEN)

BUT THE TRUTH IS THAT BOTH OF THEM LIVED IN SIMPLE STYLE WITH THE REST OF THE ORDINARY FOLK OF NAZARETH

TRANSPORT & GENERAL WORKERS
THURS 19
BR MEETING

AND THINGS LOOK DIFFERENT WHEN YOU LIVE IN CORONATION ST.

REFLECTION Nº1

HOW DIFFERENT THEOLOGY WOULD BE IF THEOLOGIANS HAD TO SUPPORT A WIFE AND FAMILY ON $35 A WEEK.

SOMETIMES YOU HEAR THAT THE RICH SHOULD GIVE THEIR EXCESS TO THE POOR. WHEN DID YOU EVER HEAR A RICH MAN SAYING HE HAD TOO MUCH MONEY?

And as for so-called Christian Social Doctrine, I don't know where they got it from, but JC himself always called a needle a needle, and a camel a camel.......

WOE TO YOU WHO SPEND $500 A YEAR ON A POODLE AND PUT A NICKEL IN THE COLLECTION BOX.

WHY SHOULD A RICH MAN WANT TO CHANGE THE WORLD?

BUT GOD DOES WANT TO CHANGE THE WORLD

THEREFORE GOD ISN'T ON THE SIDE OF THE RICH

IT'S AS EASY AS THAT.

NB WHENEVER THE WORD "RICH" CROPS UP IN THIS CHAPTER, DON'T JUST THINK THAT MEANS OTHER PEOPLE. WE ARE ALL TOO RICH AT TIMES (EG. DID YOU REALLY NEED TO BUY THIS BOOK?)

138

OTHERS TRIED A SOFTER APPROACH

I HAVEN'T COME TO SUPPORT THIS SORT OF PEACE.
TO HELL* WITH THIS —

AND DAMN THOSE WHO
PALM OFF THE REDUNDANT WITH
A BIDDING-PRAYER

* HE REALLY SAID 'SWORD' INSTEAD OF HELL, BUT WE DON'T USE SWORDS NOWADAYS, DO WE ?

Scene 1

There was once a poor devil called Lazarus covered all over in sores and lice who sometimes sat on the steps of a city bank hoping for a few shekels to buy a cuppa tea.

Every morning the Bank Manager Mr D. Ives (D = Dai; he was born in Swansea) arrived promptly at 11·13 in his limousine

– Spare a copper for a guy, Dai

–Get off my bloody steps, you alcoholic layabout, or I'll call the police ......

....It was a November night.

They both died-Lazarus of pneumonia, D Ives of liver cirrhosis
Lazarus received an all-in voucher for indefinite holidays
(Super Executive Class) in the heavenly holiday camp,
while Ives was sewing mailbags and painting bedrooms
day and night.

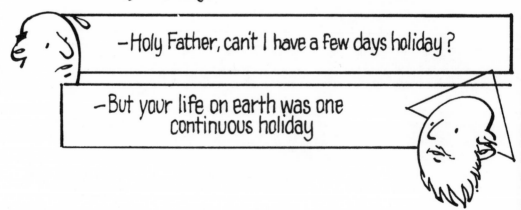

—Holy Father, can't I have a few days holiday?

—But your life on earth was one
continuous holiday

Can't you send Lazarus to buy me a rum-and-coke?

—What with? Pyjama buttons? You never gave me so much as a useless foreign coin when I used to sit outside your bank.

—If only my shareholders knew of all this: can't you tell them before it's too late!

Look here, my son — THE GOSPEL IS CLEAR AS DAY ON THIS QUESTION: it even gives you definite examples. Let your shareholders read MATTHEW 25, the final Examination.....

THE FINAL EXAM

The curtain opens, and JC (wearing his best jeans) is seen in the middle of a huge crowd divided into 2 groups. He begins speaking to one of the groups (left or right, depends which side you're looking from)

— You people didn't know how to live, did you?

It seems you didn't live out your lives in the way you were meant to. You were surrounded by death and poverty, and you went through life as if you didn't see anything yourselves. (JC starts pointing at individuals)

— One day I came to borrow a pint of milk and a loaf of bread and **you** told me you didn't believe in borrowing and lending. I lived next door to you, and you didn't want to know.

— Another day **you** in the pin-stripe suit gossiped about my clothes.

"Looks as if he buys them at the OXFAM shop" you said. You forgot I'd been made redundant and was living off Social Security.

— I finished my days in a geriatric nursing home, and **you** in the blue skirt were my daughter, and it obviously pained you to visit me for half-an-hour a fortnight. I'd brought you into the world and you made me feel useless and a nuisance!

At that point one of the accused interrupted:
— I think you've made a mistake, sir. With all respect to

QUESTIONNAIRE 1

1. How much do you enjoy living?
   a) very much
   b) depends on the day of the week
   c) not much
   d) we're not meant to enjoy life, are we?
   e) don't know

2. What do you do to create life around you?
   a) I watch a lot of telly
   b) I like to be first with the latest trends
   c) I consider other people's lives as part of my own
   d) I don't understand the question
   e) nothing

yourself and no harm intended, I never once saw you in all my life.

— He's right (said someone else); you never lived in our town. Then JC answered (well you know what he answered):

— Don't you realise, that while there was just one ill or lonely person in your town I couldn't be healthy or happy?

— You with the white trousers, you so easily switched off the "Appeal for the Week" and opened a second bottle of whisky, without asking yourself whether you could help.

—You over there in the corner, you used to laugh at the "do-gooders" in your town; but you were a "do-nothing" yourself.

— You in the green pullover, you were always shouting for longer and stricter prison sentences, but you never once entered a prison to see what it was like, nor did you ever see or visit a prisoner.

And now JC looks at the other group. He immediately relaxes, looks at them with great affection, even lights up a cigarette (Govt Health Warning: Smoking Can Seriously Endanger Your Life) in his excitement and happiness. He talks with them...

Hello my buddies, bosom pals, sweethearts... it's lovely to see you all. You are as welcome as the flowers in May, and I hope you'll all stay around for a long, long time... there's no lack of beds or food or drink. When I was with you, you treated me well, like a king in fact.(The Last Sunday in October is the Feast of Christ the King, editor's note).

Then one of his listeners jumps to his feet and challenges JC:
— Excuse me correcting you, sir, but I believe you must be

3. Are you aware of the following situations of suffering & death?
   a) what it means to be a mongol
   b) extreme shyness, to the point of having no friends
   c) a husband and wife who only keep together "for the sake of the children"
   d) a priest who is losing his faith
   e) the millions of children who will go to bed hungry tonight

QUESTIONNAIRE 2
1. How do you imagine Jesus Christ?
   a) as a Superman
   b) I don't
   c) in agony on a cross
   d) laughing his head off
   e) like a Sloane Ranger
   f) Rastafarian

thinking of another group of people. None of us ever knew you. (Then JC answers the man... well you know what he answered)

—You're the one who is mistaken, my lad. Because every time you did something for people worse off than yourself you were really doing it for me. I was there all the time.

(But now a convinced atheist jumps to his feet)

—At least **I'm** an exception to that, sir. I always did things for my fellow human-beings. I never believed in God or religion. (Those near him try to make him sit down. "Be quiet, you'll lose heaven saying things like that!" But JC answers him:

—Well now, your intellectual pride has burst like a balloon, my son. It was always your principal fault, but you made up for it by the way you looked after me in the poor, the political prisoners, and all the rest. Welcome home!

BACKGROUND MUSIC BEGINS TO SWELL (SUGGEST EITHER BEETHOVEN'S NINTH OR "ALL YOU NEED IS LOVE" BY THE BEATLES) ON ONE SIDE, AND TEETH-GNASHING SOUNDS ON THE OTHER.

JUST BEFORE THE CURTAINS CLOSE, GOD THE FATHER GOES UP TO THE TEETH-GNASHERS AND SAYS TO THEM:

—I couldn't bear to think of you all roasting in the fires of hell. I'll see you all again when I've finished looking at "Coronation Street".

AND NOW THE CURTAINS REALLY DO CLOSE, AND YOU CAN READ ON THEM
"THE END"
AND IN SMALL PRINT "ANY RESEMBLANCE TO REAL-LIFE PERSONS IS COMPLETELY AND ENTIRELY INTENTIONAL."

---

2. How many pairs of trousers do you own? (skirts or slacks in the case of girls)

    a) 8

    b) 20

    c) 1

    d) none

    e) more than I need

3. How do you understand "being a Christian"?

    a) a comfort

    b) a nuisance

    c) I don't think I am a Christian

    d) a way of life that brings me happiness

    e) any other ideas?

QUESTIONNAIRE 3

1. My friends are:
   a) all important people
   b) all unimportant people
   c) I don't have any real friends
   d) very different from each other
   e) what's it got to do with you, anyway?

2. What are you doing about your next-door failures?
   a) I'm writing a marvellous book about them
   b) I think it's their fault
   c) there's nowt so queer as folk, is my philosophy
   d) live and let live
   e) I think a lot about them and look for opportunities to be available if they need me

3. What are you doing here and now about Jesus of Nazareth?
   a) I'm writing a marvellous book about him
   b) I don't really know him very well
   c) I'd like to experience him more in the future
   d) At least I'm reading this book about him
   e) I'm frightened he'll upset my plans for enjoying life

MORAL
EVEN DEAD DOGS CAN SWIM WITH THE STREAM

IT'S NOT SURPRISING THAT WHAT JC SAID TO US MADE US FEEL SO GOOD, BECAUSE WHAT HE SAID WAS (FOR US) VERY GOOD NEWS

IT'S ALL GOING TO CHANGE : THOSE WHO ARE NOW LAUGHING UP THEIR SLEEVES WILL ONE DAY WEEP AND CRY

(AND THEY WON'T BE JUST CROCODILE TEARS, EITHER)

He was always encouraging us :

I ASSURE YOU THAT EVEN THE HAIRS ON YOUR HEAD ARE NUMBERED, AND GOD IS CONCERNED FOR EVERY SPARROW THAT CHIRPS.

SO DON'T BE AFRAID OF ANYTHING; HOWEVER DEPRESSED YOU FEEL YOURSELF TO BE, YOU'RE ALWAYS WORTH MORE THAN A SPARROW

DON'T BE RUTHLESS AND STONY-HEARTED.
KILL THE EXPLOITING SYSTEM, BUT NOT
THE PERSON RESPONSIBLE FOR IT. DON'T PULL UP THE FLOWERS
ALONG WITH THE STINGING-NETTLES

Love your enemies

BUT ABOVE ALL, LOVE THE WILL OF GOD, WHICH IS THAT ALL PEOPLE
SHOULD HAVE AN EQUAL CHANCE OF HAPPINESS.

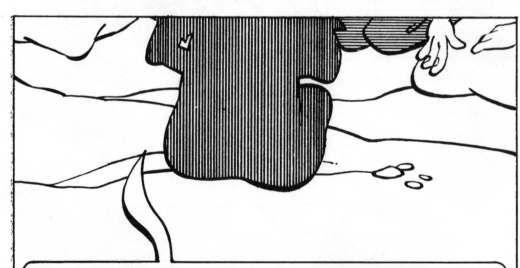

BE PURE AND SINGLE-HEARTED IN YOUR ATTEMPTS TO SHARE
LIFE AND JOY. DON'T PULL DOWN TYRANTS JUST IN ORDER TO
REPLACE THEM WITH YOURSELVES.
For the way you judge other people
will be the way you will eventually be judged.

At the same time **JC** was a realist, and knew that his followers would suffer because of their efforts.......

THEY'LL ATTACK YOU

THEY'LL IMPRISON YOU

THEY'LL TORTURE YOU

EVEN THE OFFICIAL CHURCHES WILL CONDEMN YOU

THEY'LL CALL YOU EVERY NAME UNDER THE SUN, AND WHEN YOU OPEN YOUR MOUTHS TO DEFEND YOURSELVES THEY'LL CALL YOU COMMUNISTS (AS IF THAT WERE AN INSULT)

BUT DON'T WORRY—

THEY EVEN CALLED GOD **SATAN!**

JC asked us:

ARE YOU PACKING YOUR BAGS AS WELL?

And Pete (short for 'impetuous') answered for us all:

WITH YOU WE'LL KEEP RIGHT ON TO THE END OF THE ROAD!

JC knew that a lot of people found him too radical.....

—I'M FULLY AWARE THAT NO POLITICAL PARTY WOULD EVER DARE TO FOLLOW THIS LINE, BUT IT'S UP TO US TO PICK UP OUR CROSS EVERY DAY AND GO AHEAD. IF THEY NEVER CRITICISE YOU, IF THEY RECOMMEND YOU FOR QUEEN'S BIRTHDAY HONOURS, IF THEY INVITE YOU TO THEIR BANQUETS, THAT'S ALL BECAUSE YOU'VE BECOME LIKE THEM, AND NOTHING WILL EVER REALLY CHANGE. I BELIEVE THAT BECAUSE OF ALL THIS, LOSING YOUR LIFE IS THE ONLY SURE WAY OF WINNING IT.

JC managed to get the backs up of most of the "establishment" at one time or another.......

HE'S EITHER POSSESSED BY THE DEVIL AND NEEDS EXORCISING, OR HE'S JUST A JUMPED-UP PARAPSYCHOLOGIST

IF PEOPLE LISTEN TO WHAT HE SAYS ABOUT MONEY, WE'LL NEVER ARRIVE AT THE PERFECT CAPITALIST STATE

IT'S A PITY HE DIDN'T HAVE TO DO HIS NATIONAL SERVICE

THEY ALL UNDERSTOOD THAT **JC'S** TEACHING WOULD LEAD LOGICALLY TO A REBELLION, AND IN THE END THEY SHUT HIM UP IN THE ONLY WAY THEY KNEW HOW — BUT MORE OF THAT LATER.

LISTEN, DAD
(a prayer for the young at heart)

Dear Father,
You are the one who calls us all
to live like brothers and sisters -

OUR FATHER (great cheers, applause and shouts of approval)

You are above our petty divisions — black & white, rich & poor,
handsome & plain, brain & brawn, tories & socialists, young &
old —

YOU ARE IN HEAVEN

We belong to you. You give meaning and purpose to our lives. You
are our future, and one day we'll be really close to you, for ever —

BLESS YOU!

But you know how things are at the moment...
There's a lot of pain and suffering, people dying of loneliness and
hunger; there's a lot of cruelty and exploitation going on, and it
hurts to see it all —

LET YOUR KINGDOM COME — soon! (JC says: 'only
when all the devils have left the world' •
Mrs O'Flaherty says: 'Sshh! We're supposed to be praying!)

May the
world be a bit more like you want it to be, like your dream for us
all. A bit more laughter, not so many tears. It must be one big
party in heaven with everybody united, no bickering, envy,
keeping up with the Joneses —

**LET YOUR WILL BE DONE HERE ON EARTH
AS THEY'RE DOING IT IN HEAVEN**

We can get by on very little really. We don't need all the junk food they keep showing us on telly...

GIVE US EACH DAY THE BREAD WE NEED

(the music now changes to a minor key)

OK Lord, now comes the bad part. We're to blame for a lot of the mess we're in. We're so petty, jealous, self-centred. We're so slow to forgive, and we're like elephants when it comes to never forgetting. Let's wipe the slate clean then, so that you can begin all over again with us —

FORGIVE US AND WE'LL TRY TO FORGIVE OTHERS

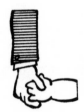

Now that we're forgiven, we can really change the world; Lord. But let the change be real and deep, not just us taking over the power from the rich and becoming like them, which would defeat you whole purpose —

DON'T LET US FALL INTO TEMPTATION

(The following is said in an undertone like a whisper from a child when the lights suddenly dim)
The truth is that things are complicated, and life isn't easy. We've all got our weaknesses and problems, and sometimes we are overcome by darkness when we want to walk in the light —

DELIVER US FROM WHAT IS EVIL

LET ALL THIS BE TRUE ! IT **WILL** BE BECAUSE YOU WANT I
TO BE! A BIG HUG FROM ALL YOUR CHILDREN !

JC WAS A FIGHTER ALL RIGHT—
BUT DON'T IMAGINE HIM AS A LONG-FACED LOONY
WITH A CHIP ON HIS SHOULDER;
HE STRUGGLED TO BRING MORE <u>LIFE</u> INTO
THE WORLD, BECAUSE :

Kingdom= life ✝ Liberty

I ONCE HAD A FRIEND CALLED FRED—A TREMENDOUS GUY. BUT HE HAD THE BAD LUCK TO INHERIT A (MIS) FORTUNE, AND HE CHANGED OVERNIGHT.

JC SAID TO HIM:
GIVE IT AWAY TO THE POOR, FRED, OR TO SAVE THE CHILDREN — IF YOU WANT TO STAY WITH US, THAT IS.

BECAUSE EVERY MAN HAS HIS PRIORITIES IN LIFE, AND THAT'S WHERE HE PUTS HIS HEART.

FRED KEPT HIS MONEY AND LEFT OUR GANG.... HE BECAME A PROPERTY SPECULATOR AND TODAY HE SPEAKS IN CLICHÉS, LIKE "TIME IS MONEY" AND "I DIDN'T GET WHERE I AM TODAY"....

DON'T GIVE TOO MUCH IMPORTANCE TO BIG WORDS, HIGH IDEALS AND GREAT GOALS, WHEN THEY STOP YOU TASTING THE LITTLE EVERYDAY PLEASURES GOD HAS PREPARED FOR YOU.

E.G.1
be simple in your words – say 'yes' or 'no' without complications.

Lying enslaves you.
The truth makes you free.

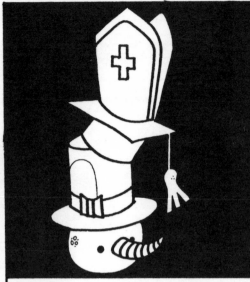

E.G.2
be simple in your titles – avoid 'Worshipful Honours', 'Most Reverend Eminences', etc.

E.G.3
be simple in your relationships – don't judge others; everyone is basically lovable. Love your enemies.

E.G.4
be simple in your beliefs and ideologies: the individual is more important than the state; love is bigger than the family. Treat others as you expect them to treat you.

WE KEPT WITH **JC** BECAUSE WE FELT WE WERE REALLY GOING SOMEWHERE WITH HIM, EVEN THOUGH THERE WERE TIMES WHEN WE DIDN'T HAVE THE PRICE OF BED AND BREAKFAST BETWEEN US.

THE REASON WHY I'M HERE IS SO THAT YOU CAN ALL HAVE **LIFE** IN ALL ITS FULNESS, SO THAT THE BLIND CAN SEE, THE CRIPPLES RECOVER THEIR HEALTH, THE DUMB SHOUT FOR JOY AND SO THAT EVERYBODY CAN BE PROMOTED TO THE FIRST DIVISION.

174

DON'T BELITTLE YOUR TALENTS:
WHAT I'VE TOLD YOU IN SECRET IS WORTH SHOUTING OUT AT SPEAKERS CORNER OR SINGING ABOUT AT CARNEGIE HALL

LUCKY
are those who live in Shanty Town
because God comes to eat in their homes

LUCKY

are those who feel the suffering of others
because they'll be over the moon when all
suffering comes to an end

LUCKY
are those who resist the call of violence
(even when they are called 'pansies' or 'poofs')
because they are the **real** he-men of the world

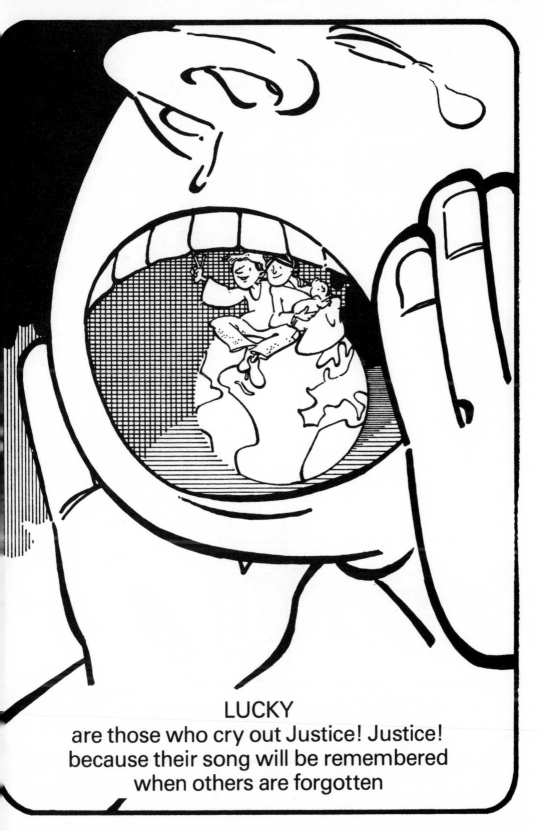

LUCKY
are those who cry out Justice! Justice!
because their song will be remembered
when others are forgotten

LUCKY
are those who support the underdog
and share his life's worries
because they are on the fast lane to God

LUCKY
are those who keep an open mind and
a clean heart, because they will come to
understand things as they really are

LUCKY
are those whose deepest yearnings
are for peace, because God himself
has taken root in them

LUCKY
are you who are made to lead a dog's life
because of your love of truth; a day
will come when God will wipe away your tears

LUCKY
are you who are driven from your
homes and families because of me:
you are on the road to your real home

and LUCKY
are those who are never
ashamed of me

the sky is red

red sky at night christians delight!